MW01153923

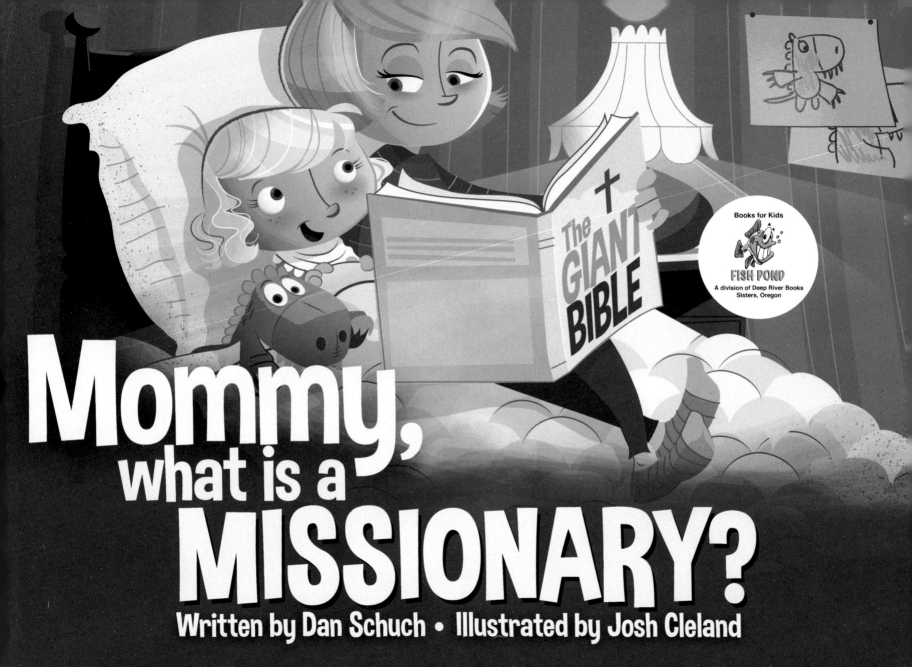

The GIANT BIBLE

Books for Kids

FISH POND
A division of Deep River Books
Sisters, Oregon

Mommy, what is a MISSIONARY?

Written by Dan Schuch • Illustrated by Josh Cleland

FishPond is an imprint of Deep River Books. The views expressed or implied in this work are those of the author. To learn more about Deep River Books, go online to www.DeepRiverBooks.com.

ISBN 13: 978-1-63269-385-3
Library of Congress Catalog Card Number: 2014939822

Dedication

To missionaries worldwide who give and sacrifice so much in order that everyone may experience God's never-ending love for them, and with much love to Nancy, Katie, and Matthew, whose lives of sacrifice are an inspiration to me.—DS

To my wonderful parents, who encouraged my wacky childhood ambition to become an illustrator and cartoonist, and to Rayna, my amazing wife, to whom I owe my entire career.—JC

Mommy, what is a missionary?
Well, Katie, a missionary is a
person like you and me.

Some missionaries are men, ...

and some missionaries are women.

Some are married,
and some are single.

Some like cats,

some like dogs, ...

DOG PARK

8

nd many like both!

Some missionaries like to read, some like to fish,...

and some like to go for walks.

CAMP ZIG ZAG

11

Some like pie,

and some like ice cream.

12

Others like hamburgers, and salads.

Many missionaries like to try new foods.

Some missionaries like to sing, others like to dance, and some like tennis.

Some are graceful,

some
are
clumsy,

and some like to paint.

15

Some missionaries are tall, and some are short.

Some live in the city,

and some live in the country.

17

Some missionaries are parents,

some are not,

and some are grandparents.

Some live in the United States,

and some live in other countries.

19

but all missionaries love boys and
girls like you, Katie!

21

All missionaries love Jesus.

All missionaries love to learn about Jesus by reading the Bible.

And Jesus loves all missionaries very much!

Because some people do not know that Jesus loves them, all missionaries want to tell others about Jesus.

Katie, did you know that all missionaries also love to pray for you and me?

24

Mommy, is it OK if I pray for the missionaries too?

Yes, Katie. They would really like that.
And so would our heavenly Father.

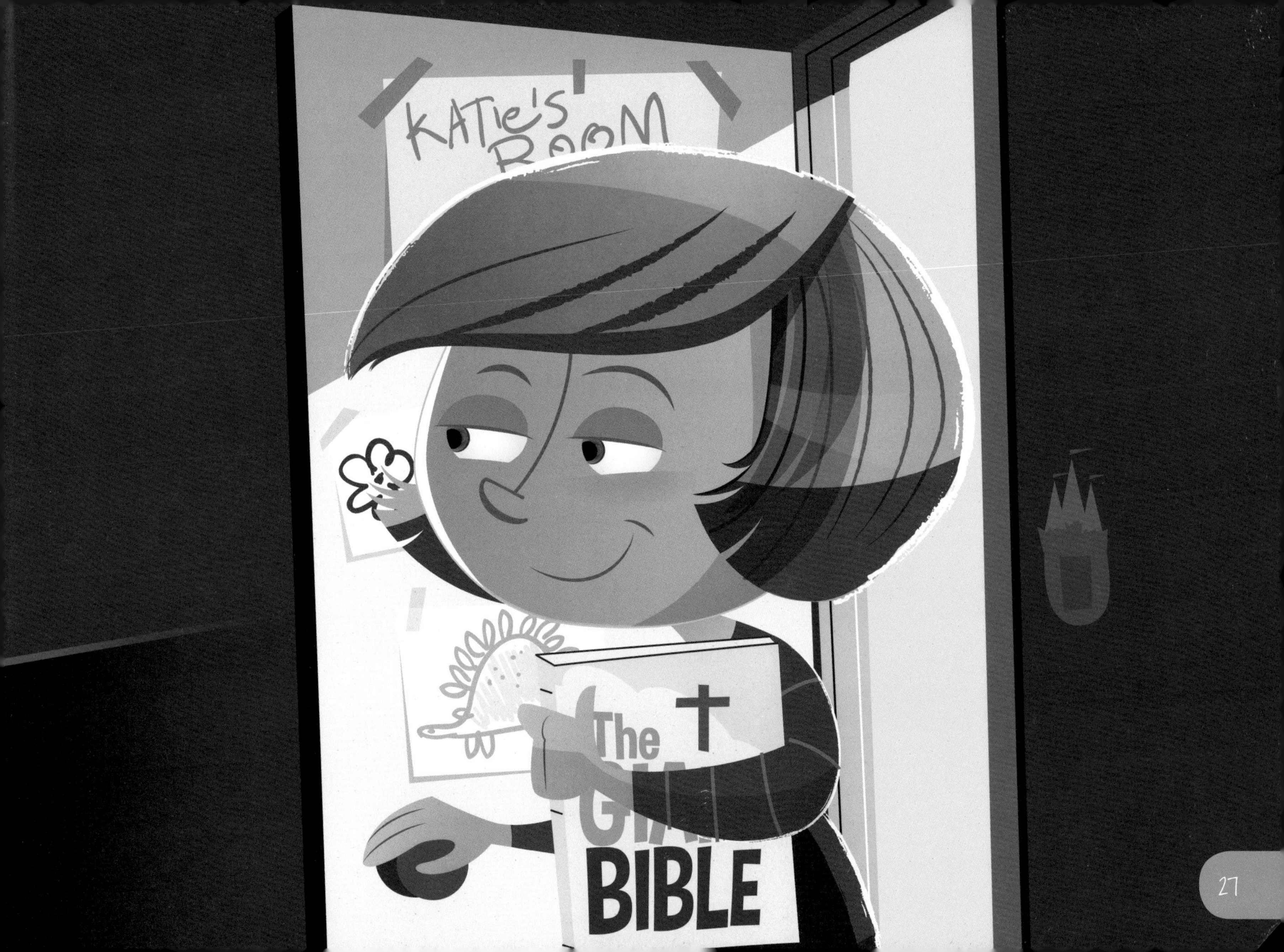
KATie's ROOM
The
BIBLE

Notes for Parents and Teachers

This book is designed so you can interact with a child in various ways. On each page of the text, you will find questions, some that encourage creativity and others that probe and develop spiritual truths. Use these questions as a guide, or ask some of your own questions to spark meaningful conversations about God, Jesus, and missionaries as you read.

Pg. 4 Some missionaries are men,...

What is the missionary doing? What Bible story is he telling the children? How many boys and girls do you see?

Pg. 5 and some missionaries are women.

How many tools are in the picture?

What is the missionary building?

Pg. 6 Some are married, and some are single.

What did the single missionary eat for dinner?

The single missionary appears to be using a highlighter. Is it OK to write in the Bible?

Pg. 7 Some are older, and some are younger.

Why do you think they are digging?

Where do you think they are?

Pg. 8 Some like cats, some like dogs,...

How many cats are in the picture?

Which dog is your favorite? Why?

Pg. 9 and many like both!

What do you think they are doing on the beach?

Do you like to go to the beach?

28

Pg. 10 Some like to read, some like to fish.

How many books are in the boat?

What is the name of the boat?

Pg. 11 And some like to go for walks.

What are they doing while they are walking?

What do they have around their necks?

Pg. 12 Some like pie, and some like ice cream.

Which do you like better, pie or ice cream?

For whom is the missionary baking the pie?

Pg. 13 Others like hamburgers, and salads. Many missionaries like to try new foods.

What new food is the missionary going to eat?

What is your favorite food?

Pg. 14 Some missionaries like to sing, others like to dance, and some like tennis.

What is your favorite song?

Do you like to dance?

Pg. 15 Some are graceful, some are clumsy, and some like to paint.

What is your favorite thing to do?

Have you ever been clumsy?

Pg. 16 Some missionaries are tall, and some are short.

What kind of missionaries do you think these are?

Have you ever wanted a bunny rabbit?

Pg. 17 Some live in the city, some live in the country.

Have you ever fed ducks or geese?
Would you like to do this?

Have you ever petted a goat?

Pg. 18 Some missionaries are parents, some are not, and some are grandparents.

Do you think missionary kids are missionaries too?

How old does a missionary have to be?

29

Pg. 19 Some live in the United States, and some live in other countries.

(Use a map for this activity.)
Let's find where we live on this map.
Where do other members of our family live?

Do we know someone who lives in another country?

Pg. 20 Some work in an office, and some don't,...

Would you like to pet a camel?

Where would you like to work when you grow up?

Pg. 21 but all missionaries love boys and girls like you, Katie!

Missionaries can have many differences, but let's name some of the things they have in common as we read the rest of the book.

Pg. 22 All missionaries love Jesus... and Jesus loves all missionaries very much.

The Bible teaches us who Jesus is and what he is like. Jesus loves you, and Jesus loves me.

Pg. 23 Because some people do not know that Jesus loves them, all missionaries want to tell others about Jesus.

(This gets to the heart of the purpose and definition of a missionary. Spend some time talking about this.) What do you think is the most important thing a missionary does?

Pg. 24 Katie, did you know that all missionaries also love to pray for you and me?

What do you think it means to pray? Yes, praying is simply talking to God.

Pg. 25 Mommy, is it OK if I pray for the missionaries too?

We can pray for God to help and protect the missionaries. Would you like to do that right now?

Pg. 26 Katie praying.

Talk to the child about praying for missionaries.

Acknowledgements

Thank you to my wife, Chaleen, for her support and love in spite of my numerous flaws, and for her deep passion and commitment to missions; and to the loving, Almighty God and my Lord and Savior, Jesus Christ,

- for my redemption,

- for showing favor and bringing me a partner, my wife, Chaleen,

- for honoring and entrusting me with this book project,

- for bringing Josh into the picture, one who chooses to honor you with his incredible skills, and

- for providing mentors Eldridge, Miller, Brown, and Langston to guide and inspire me.

—*Dan Schuch*

I would like to thank Dan and Chaleen for the amazing opportunity to illustrate this wonderful project and for their patience while the book was being illustrated. I also acknowledge the Almighty God for his amazing timing in bringing this project to fruition. Dan began talking with me nearly nine years ago about this project, and having it completed is a testament to God's awesomeness.

—*Josh Cleland*

Lee Pursley

I first met Lee when I was attending seminary in Fort Worth, Texas, and he began to work at the same computer store that I did. He had just moved to Fort Worth to attend seminary after serving as a missionary in Zambia. While Lee was in Zambia, he had worked with a missionary family whose son managed the computer store where we worked.

I became fast friends with Lee. We shared many interests—theater, games, baseball, Star Trek, and a deep love for the Lord.

I was there at the beginning of Lee's courtship with Nancy and watched their relationship lead to marriage. After seminary, Lee and Nancy served as missionaries in a difficult and complex part of the world.

Tragically, Lee died from heart problems while attending a missionary conference in Thailand. He left behind his wife, a four-year-old daughter, and a ten-month-old son.

I was asked to speak at Lee's funeral. The night before I spoke, I had a vision from God—this book. The entire book was presented to me in my head. When I woke up, I sketched out the book. Almost ten years to the day that Lee passed away, work began to complete this project commissioned by God. Part of the proceeds from this book will go toward a college fund for Lee's children, Katie and Matthew.

I believe that God wants our children to know about and pray for our missionaries. All of those who have endeavored to produce this book pray that it will help in this regard.

—Dan Schuch